Chameleons

are amazing reptiles

I0410081

Deep in the heart of the Sahara Desert is a semi-nomadic tribe who is learning to read and write their language for the first time in their history.

Your purchase of this book is supporting the transformation of these communities through this emerging literacy movement.

Chameleons can do some surprising things.

**Chameleons can
change the color
of their skin.**

A chameleon's changing skin color can help scare away an enemy.

When he is hot he can make his skin a lighter color. When he is cold he can make his skin darker.

He can make himself colorful to attract a female.

He can change his color to blend in with the things around him.

In the blink of
an eye he can
shoot out his
tongue to catch
a fly.

Chameleons eat flies, beetles and other insects.

Chameleons can move their eyes in different directions to see more than one thing at the same time.

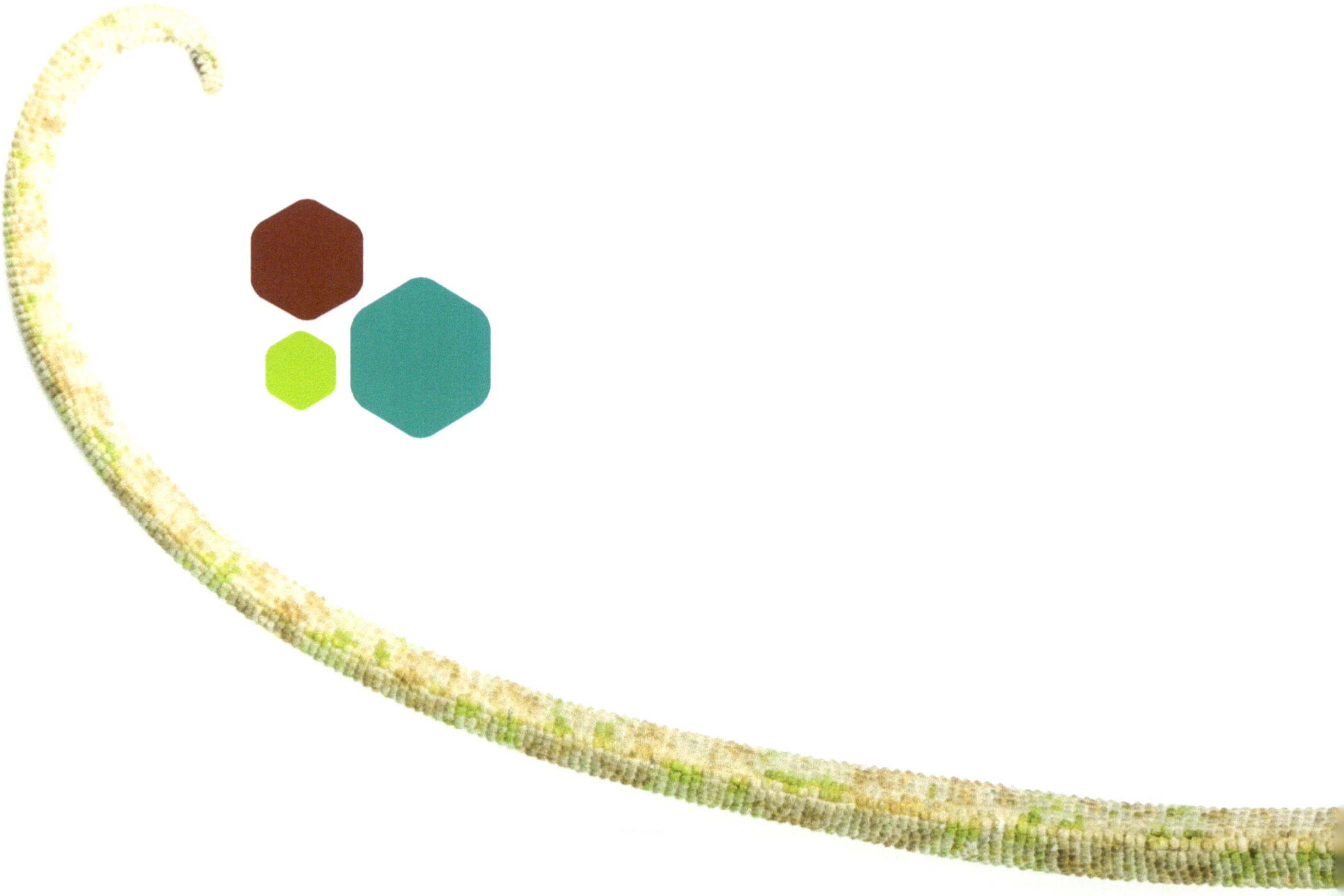

Chameleons have very strong toes to grip and climb up tiny branches.

Chameleons can also use their tails to hold onto branches.

Chameleons live in many places.

Mountains

Forests

Grasslands

Swamps

Cities

Chameleons are reptiles and have things in common with:

Monitor Lizards

Snakes

Turtles

Crocodiles

Lizards

Can you guess how they are similar?

All reptiles lay
soft-shelled
eggs.

They are cold-blooded and love laying in the sun.

They have rough, scaly skin.

An story from the Sahara Desert describing how slow chameleons are.

One day Papa Chameleon's children were hungry. He left to go find something for the children to eat. After waiting a long time the children looked out to see if their father had returned. Seeing him far off, they began yelling, "Dad's back, dad's back!"

Papa Chameleon answered back "I am just now leaving, how could I be coming back already?"

25

Produced by APE (Association pour la Promotion de l'Education)
Text by Armi Mamar, Mohamed Abakar, and Rivers Camp (Galmai Wûji)
Layout Design by Robert Johnson (Sûmpi Zen)

yagabi

Published by Yagabi ©2014
All Rights Reserved
yagabibooks@gmail.com

www.ingramcontent.com/pod-product-compliance
Lightning Source LLC
Chambersburg PA
CBHW060813290526

45792CB00005BA/1639

* 9 7 8 1 5 3 5 2 0 1 6 7 4 *